GUITAR • VOCAL

STRUM & SING

ADELE

Lyrics, Chord Symbols and Guitar Chord Frames for 13 Hit Songs

Photo credit: Mari Sarii

ISBN 978-1-4950-6322-0

HAL•LEONARD®
CORPORATION
7777 W. BLUEMOUND RD. P.O. BOX 13819 MILWAUKEE, WI 53213

Visit Hal Leonard Online at
www.halleonard.com

CONTENTS

All I Ask

Words and Music by Adele Adkins,
Philip Lawrence, Bruno Mars
and Chris Brown

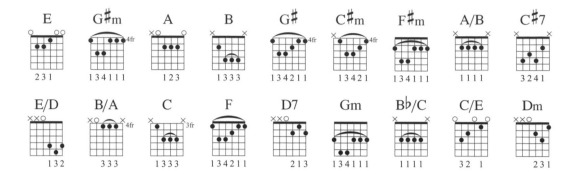

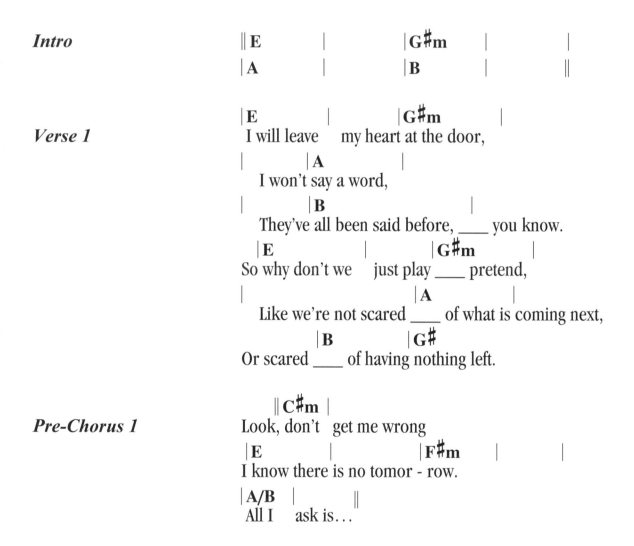

Intro

|| E | |G♯m | |
|A | |B | ||

Verse 1

|E | |G♯m |
I will leave   my heart at the door,
| |A |
   I won't say a word,
| |B |
   They've all been said before, ___ you know.
|E | |G♯m |
So why don't we   just play ___ pretend,
| |A |
   Like we're not scared ___ of what is coming next,
|B |G♯ |
Or scared ___ of having nothing left.

Pre-Chorus 1

|| C♯m |
Look, don't get me wrong
|E | |F♯m | |
I know there is no tomor - row.
|A/B | ||
All I   ask is…

Chorus 1

```
|E    |            |C#7 |            |F#m   |        |
   If    this is my last     night with you
|A/B                    |B            |E        |
Hold me like I'm more ___ than just a friend.
|             |C#7   |    |F#m   |        |
    Give me a mem'ry I can  use,
|A/B                    |B            |E        |B    |C#m
 Take me by the hand ___ while we do what lovers do,
|                       |F#m       |
It matters how this ends.
|         |A/B                    |        ||
     'Cause what if I never love again?
```

Interlude   *Repeat Intro*

Verse 2

```
|E             |        |G#m         |
 I don't need    your hon - esty,
|                |A            |
   It's already in your eyes
|          |B                |            |
   And I'm sure my eyes, they speak for me.
|E             |            |G#m         |
 No one knows    me like ___ you do
|                          |A          |
   And since you're the only one that matters
                    |B          |G#
Tell me who ___ do I run to?
```

Pre-Chorus 2   *Repeat Pre-Chorus 1*

5

Chorus 2

```
|E              |C#7  |          |F#m    |        |
   If    this is my last     night with you
|A/B                |B          |E        |
Hold me like I'm more ___ than just a friend.
|              |C#7   |    |F#m    |        |
     Give me a mem'ry I can  use,
|A/B              |B          |E        |B    |C#m
Take me by the hand ___ while we do what lovers  do,
|                      |F#m        |
It matters how this ends.
|          |A/B              |            ||
     'Cause what if I never love ___ again?
```

Bridge

```
|E/D    |               |A       | G#m |F#m    |
              Let this be our lesson ___  in       love,
|                 |A/B  |B     B/A  |G#m      |
     Let this be the way we ___ re - member us.
|                   |G#    |     |C#m    |
     I don't wanna be cruel   or  vi - cious
|              |F#m              |        |
     And I ain't asking for forgive - ness.
|A/B    |     C ||
All I    ask...
```

Chorus 3

```
|F     |          |D7    |         |Gm       |        |
   If    this is my last     night with  you
|Bb/C                    |C            |F        |
Hold me like I'm more ___ than just a  friend.
|          |D7      |        |Gm       |        |
     Give me a mem'ry ___ I can  use,
|Bb/C            |C           |F      |C/E  |Dm
Take me by the hand while we do what lovers  do,
|                          |Gm        |
It matters how this ends.
|          |Bb/C              |        |        |    |F      ||
     'Cause what if I never love _____ a - gain?
```

Hello

Words and Music by
Adele Adkins and Greg Kurstin

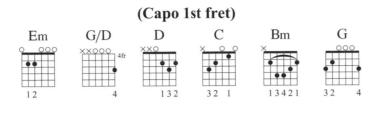

(Capo 1st fret)

Em   G/D   D   C   Bm   G

Intro

| Em   G/D | D   C

Verse 1

|| Em G/D | D   C
Hel - lo,   it's me.
| Em   G/D | D
I was won - dering if after all these years
        C | Em G/D | D   C
You'd like to meet to go o - ver   everything.
                        | Em   G/D
They say that time's ___ supposed to heal ya,
| D   C
But I ain't done much healing.

Verse 2

|| Em G/D | D   C
Hel - lo,   can you hear ___ me?
| Em   G/D | D   C
I'm in Cal - ifor - nia, dreaming about who ___ we used to be
                        | Em G/D | D   C
When we were young - er   and free.
        | Em   G/D | D   C
I've forgot - ten how it felt before the world ___ fell at our ___ feet.
                    | Em   D | Bm   C
There's such a diff'rence   be - tween us
| Em   D   C | ||
And a milli - on miles.

```
Em          C              |G    D
Hello from the other side.
|Em            C              |G    D
I must have called a thousand times
        |Em    C            |G          D
To tell you ___ I'm sorry for ev'ry - thing that I've done
                |Em    C  |G        D    |
But when I call ___ you never seem to be home.
|Em         C          |G    D
 Hello from the outside.
 |Em         C              |G    D
At least I can say that I've tried
        |Em    C        |G            D
To tell you ___ I'm sorry for breaking your heart.
                |Em  C            |
But it don't mat - ter it clearly doesn't
|G           D              |Em  G/D  |D    C
 Tear you a - part anymore.
```

```
        ||Em G/D          |D          C
Hel - lo,       how are ___ you?
        |Em    G/D              |D          C
It's so typical of me to talk about ___ myself, I'm sorry.
        |Em G/D            |D    C
I hope ___       that you're well.
        |Em          G/D
Did you ev - er make it ___ out of that town
        |D            C
Where noth - ing ever ___ happened?
    |Em    D        |Bm    C
It's no secret    that the both of us
    |Em      D    C
Are running out of time.
```

‖**Em**   **C** |**G** **D**
So, hello from the other side.

|**Em**   **C** |**G** **D**
I must have called a thousand times

    |**Em** **C** |**G**   **D**
To tell you ___ I'm sorry for ev'ry - thing that I've done

       |**Em** **C** |**G**   **D** |
But when I call ___ you never seem to be home.

|**Em**   **C** |**G** **D**
 Hello from the outside.

 |**Em**   **C** |**G** **D**
At least I can say that I've tried

    |**Em** **C** |**G**   **D**
To tell you ___ I'm sorry for breaking your heart.

      |**Em** **C** |
But it don't mat - ter it clearly doesn't

|**G**   **D** |**Em** **C**
 Tear you a - part anymore.

  |**D** **G** |**Em** **C**
Ooh, _____ anymore.

  |**D** **G** |**Em** **C**
Ooh, _____ anymore.

  |**D** **G** |**Em** **C** |**D** ‖
Ooh, _____ anymore. ___ Anymore.

Em   **C** |**G** **D**
Hello from the other side.

|**Em**   **C** |**G** **D**
I must have called a thousand times

    |**Em** **C** |**G**   **D**
To tell you ___ I'm sorry for ev'ry - thing that I've done

       |**Em** **C** |**G**   **D** |
But when I call ___ you never seem to be home.

|**Em**   **C** |**G** **D**
 Hello from the outside.

 |**Em**   **C** |**G** **D**
At least I can say that I've tried

    |**Em** **C** |**G**   **D**
To tell you ___ I'm sorry for breaking your heart.

      |**Em** **C** |
But it don't mat - ter it clearly doesn't

|**G**   **D** |**Em** **G/D** |**D** **C** |**Em** ‖
 Tear you a - part anymore.

Chasing Pavements

Words and Music by
Adele Adkins and Francis Eg White

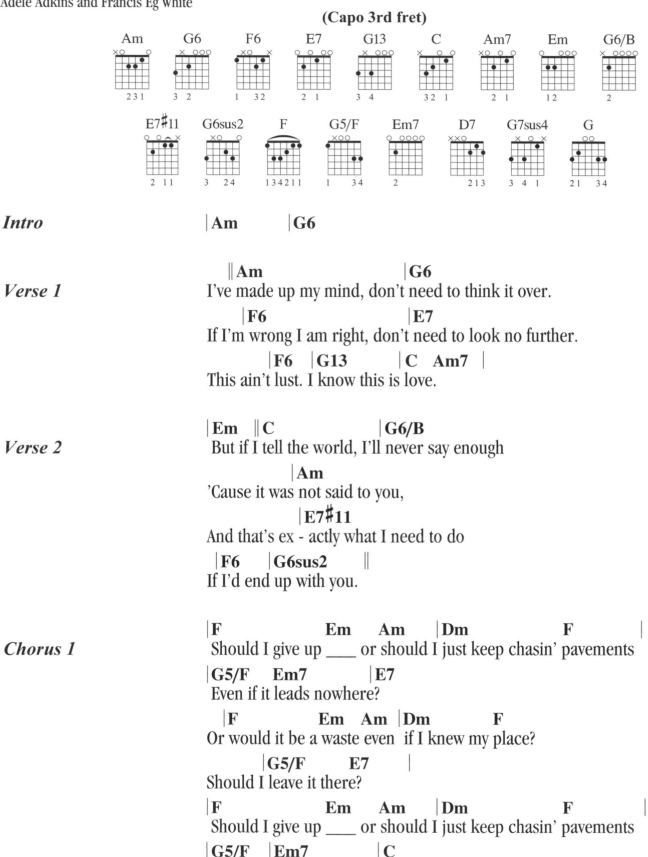

(Capo 3rd fret)

Intro |Am |G6

Verse 1
‖Am |G6
I've made up my mind, don't need to think it over.
    |F6 |E7
If I'm wrong I am right, don't need to look no further.
        |F6 |G13 |C   Am7 |
This ain't lust. I know this is love.

Verse 2
|Em   ‖C |G6/B
   But if I tell the world, I'll never say enough
                    |Am
'Cause it was not said to you,
                 |E7♯11
And that's ex - actly what I need to do
  |F6 |G6sus2   ‖
If I'd end up with you.

Chorus 1
|F   Em   Am |Dm   F |
   Should I give up ___ or should I just keep chasin' pavements
|G5/F   Em7 |E7
Even if it leads nowhere?
    |F   Em   Am |Dm   F
Or would it be a waste even if I knew my place?
          |G5/F   E7 |
Should I leave it there?
|F   Em   Am |Dm   F |
   Should I give up ___ or should I just keep chasin' pavements
|G5/F |Em7 |C
Even if it leads nowhere? Ooh.

Verse 3

‖**Am** |**G6**
I build myself up and fly around in circles,

      |**F6** |**E7**
Wait then as my heart drops and my back begins to tingle.

     |**F6** |**G6sus2**   ‖
Final - ly, could this be it? Or…

Chorus 2

|**F**   **Em**   **Am** |**Dm**   **F** |
 Should I give up ___ or should I just keep chasin' pavements

|**G5/F** |**Em7** |**E7**
 Even if it leads nowhere?

  |**F**   **Em**   **Am** |**Dm**   **F**
Or would it be a waste even if I knew my place?

      |**G5/F**   **E7** |
Should I leave it there?

|**F**   **Em**   **Am** |**Dm**   **F** |
 Should I give up ___ or should I just keep chasin' pavements

|**G/F** |**Em** |**C**   ‖
 Even if it leads nowhere? Yeah.

Chorus 3

  |**F** |**Em**
 Should I give up or should I just keep chasin' pavements

      |**F** |**G**
Even if it leads no - where?

        |**F** |**E7♯11**
Or would it be a waste even if I knew my place?

        |**D7**
Should I leave it there?

    |**G7sus4** |
Should I ___ give up or should I

|**F**   **Em** **Am** |**Dm**   **F**
 Just keep on ___ chasin' ___ pavements?

     |**Em7**   **Am** |**Dm**   **F** |**Dm**   **G**   ‖
Should I just keep on ___ chasin' ___ pavements? ___ Oh.

Outro-Chorus   *Repeat Chorus 2*

Don't You Remember

Words and Music by
Adele Adkins and Dan Wilson

(Capo 3rd fret)

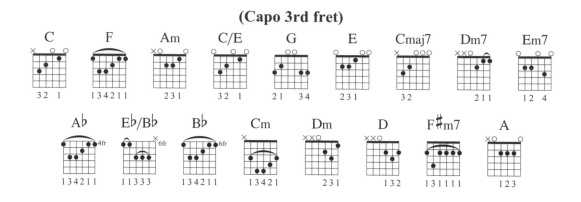

Intro
‖: C | | :‖

Verse 1
|C |F
When will I see you again?
|Am C |F
You left with no goodbye, not a single word was said.
|C C/E |F
No final kiss to seal any sins,
|Am C |F
I had no idea of the state we were in.

Pre-Chorus 1
‖ G
I know I have a fickle heart and a bitterness
|Am E |G
And a wand'ring eye and heaviness in my head.

Chorus 1
N.C. ‖C Cmaj7 |
But don't you re - member,
|F |Dm7 G |
Don't you re - member
|C F C | Em7 |F
The reason you loved me _____ be - fore?
|Dm7 G |C ‖
Baby, please remem - ber me once more.

Verse 2

```
|C                                    |F
When was the last time you thought ___ of me?
                    |Am           C              |F
Or have you com - pletely erased ___ me from your mem - ory?
        |C          C/E             |F
I often think about where I went wrong.
                    |Am   C        |F
The more I do, ___       the less I know.
```

Pre-Chorus 2

```
                                ‖G
But I know I have a fickle heart and a bitterness
        |Am                E              |G
And a wand'ring eye and heaviness in my head.
```

Chorus 2

```
N.C.                    ‖C          Cmaj7      |
    But don't you re - member,
|F                  |Dm7    G       |
    Don't you re - member
|C      F                    C   |  Em7        |F
    The reason you loved me _____ be - fore?
                        |Dm7   G          |F
Baby, please remem - ber      me once more.
```

Bridge

```
        ‖A♭                Eb/B♭
I  gave you the space so you could breathe,
            |B♭                          F
I kept my distance so you would be free,
    ‖A♭                    Cm
In hope that you'd find the missing piece
    |Dm              G       |
To bring you back to me.
```

Chorus 3

```
|2/4 N.C.            ‖4/4 D      F♯m7  |
    Why don't you re - member,
|G                  |Em7    A     |
    Don't you re - member
|D      G                    D  | F♯m7      |G
    The reason you loved me _____ be - fore?
                        |Em7      A     |G           ‖
Baby, please remem - ber me ___ once more.
```

Outro

```
|D                      |G           ‖
 When will I see you again?
```

Make You Feel My Love

Words and Music by
Bob Dylan

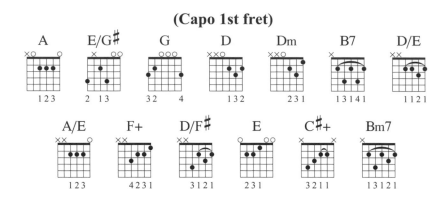

(Capo 1st fret)

Intro | A | E/G♯ | G | D |
           | Dm | A | B7 D/E | A ||

Verse 1
| A | E/G♯ |
When the rain is blowing in your face
| G | D |
And the whole world is on ____ your case,
| Dm | A |
I could offer you a warm embrace
| B7   D/E | A ||
To make you feel my love.

Verse 2
| A | E/G♯ |
When the evening shadows and the stars appear
| G | D |
And there is no one there to dry ____ your tears,
| Dm | A |
I can hold you for a million years
| B7   D/E | A ||
To make you feel my love.

Bridge 1

```
|D                              |A/E        |
    I know you haven't made your mind up yet,
|F+          D/F♯          |A              |
    But I would never do you wrong.
|D                              |A          |
    I've known it from the moment that we met,
|B7                              |E          ‖
    No doubt in my mind where you belong.
```

Verse 3

```
|A                    E/G♯          |
    I'd go hungry, I'd go black and blue,
|G                              |D          |
    I'd go crawling down the av - enue.
|Dm                        |A          |
    Know there's nothing that I wouldn't do
|B7              D/E      |A          ‖
    To make you feel my love.
```

Interlude   *Repeat Verse 1 (Instrumental)*

Bridge 2

```
|D                              |A          |
    The storms are raging on the rolling sea
|C♯+              D        |A          |
    And on the high - way of regret.
|D                              |A          |
    The winds of change are blowing wild and free.
|Bm7                        |D/E          ‖
    You ain't seen nothing like me yet.
```

Verse 4

```
|A                              |E/G♯          |
    I can make you happy, make your dreams come true.
|G                    |D          |
    Nothing that I would - n't do.
|Dm                        |A          |
    Go to the ends of the earth for you,
|B7              D/E      |A          |
    To make you feel my love,
|B7              D/E      |A          ‖
    To make you feel my love.
```

Million Years Ago

Words and Music by
Adele Adkins and Gregory Kurstin

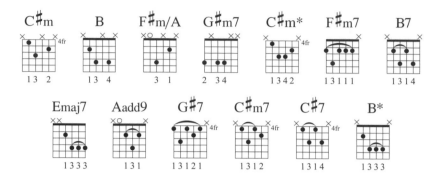

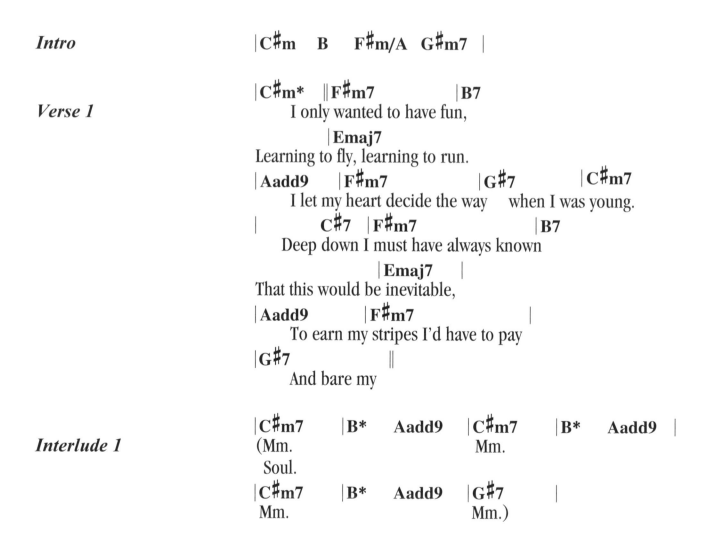

Intro

|C#m   B   F#m/A G#m7 |

Verse 1

|C#m*   ‖F#m7 |B7
    I only wanted to have fun,

      |Emaj7
Learning to fly, learning to run.

|Aadd9 |F#m7 |G#7 |C#m7
    I let my heart decide the way   when I was young.

| C#7 |F#m7 |B7
    Deep down I must have always known

       |Emaj7 |
That this would be inevitable,

|Aadd9 |F#m7 |
    To earn my stripes I'd have to pay

|G#7   ‖
    And bare my

Interlude 1

|C#m7 |B*   Aadd9 |C#m7 |B*   Aadd9 |
(Mm.   Mm.

   Soul.

|C#m7 |B*   Aadd9 |G#7 |
Mm.   Mm.)

Chorus 1

```
|                     ‖F♯m7           |B7
             I know I'm not the only one
                    |Emaj7                    |Aadd9
Who regrets ___ the things they've done.
                       |F♯m7             |
Sometimes I just feel it's only me
|G♯7                        |C♯m7          |
       Who can't stand the re - flection that they see.
  C♯7        |F♯m7           |B7
I wish I could live a little more,
                        |Emaj7            |Aadd9
Look up to the sky, not just the floor.
                     |F♯m7            |G♯7
I feel like my life is flashing by
                     |C♯m7           |
And all I can do is watch and cry.
  C♯7      |F♯m7          |B7
I miss the air, I miss my friends.
                    |Emaj7               |
I miss my moth - er. I miss it when
|Aadd9        |F♯m7                 |
     Life was a party to be thrown.
|G♯7                  |C♯m7  B    F♯m/A  G♯m7  |C♯m*        |
     But that was a mil - lion  years   a  -   go.
|        B  F♯m/A  G♯m7 |
```

Verse 2

```
|C♯m*              ‖F♯m7                    |
        When I walk a - round all of the streets
|B7            |Emaj7                |Aadd9
     Where I grew up and found my feet
             |F♯m7             |
They can't look me in the eye.
|G♯7                       |C♯m7           |
     It's like they're scared of me.
|      C♯7 |F♯m7                |B7
   I try to   think of things to say,
              |Emaj7          |Aadd9
Like a joke ___ or a memory,
                 |F♯m7             |G♯7                    ‖
But they don't recognize me now     in the light of…
```

Interlude 2

```
|C#m7        |B*    Aadd9  |C#m7        |B*    Aadd9   |
 (Mm.                       Mm.
  Day.
|C#m7        |B*    Aadd9  |G#7            |
 Mm.                        Mm.)
```

Chorus 2

```
|              ||F#m7        |B7
     I know I'm not the only one
              |Emaj7               |Aadd9
Who regrets ___ the things they've done.
              |F#m7          |
Sometimes I just feel it's only me
|G#7            |C#m7                         |
    Who never be - came who they thought would be.
 C#7        |F#m7          |B7
I wish I could live a little more,
              |Emaj7          |Aadd9
Look up to the sky, not just the floor.
              |F#m7          |G#7
I feel like my life is flashing by
              |C#m7          |
And all I can do is watch and cry.
 C#7    |F#m7          |B7
I miss the air, I miss my friends.
              |Emaj7               |
I miss my moth - er. I miss it when
|Aadd9     |F#m7                |
    Life was a party to be thrown.
|G#7            |C#m7  B   F#m/A  G#m7  |C#m*
    But that was a mil - lion  years    a  -    go.
|      B   F#m/A  G#m7 |C#m*          ||
A mil - lion years     a  -   go.
```

One and Only

Words and Music by Adele Adkins,
Dan Wilson and Greg Wells

(Capo 3rd fret)

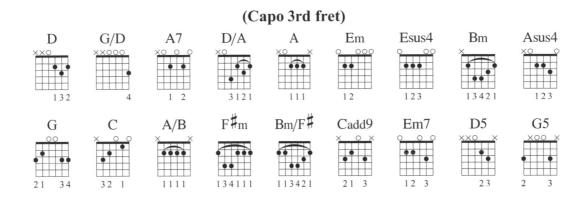

Intro | D   G/D D | A7   D/A A7

Verse 1
        ‖D   G/D D | A   D/A A
You've been on my mind   I grow fonder ev - 'ry   day,
     | Em   Esus4 Em | Bm
Lose myself in ___ time   just thinking of your face.
A | D   G/D D | A   D/A A
God only knows   why it's taken me so   long
     | Em   Esus4 Em | Bm   Asus4 A
To let my doubts ___ go,   you're the only one that I want.

Pre-Chorus 1
     ‖G   A
I don't know why I'm scared, I've been here before,
    | Bm |
Ev'ry feeling, ev'ry word, I've imagined it all.
| C |
You'll never know if you never try to
| G | Asus4   A
Forget your past and simply be mine.

Chorus 1

```
              ‖D               G/D  D            |Bm  A/B  Bm
I dare you to let me be yours,        your one and on - ly.
                   |F♯m  Bm/F♯ F♯m           |G    F♯m
I promise I'm worthy            to hold in your arms.
      Em      A     |D          G/D  D
So come on, ___ and give me the chance
                   |Bm            A/B   Bm
To prove I am the one who can
      |F♯m Bm/F♯ F♯m               |G      F♯m  Em
Walk that mile            until the end ___ starts.
```

Verse 2

```
       A            ‖D   G/D  D        |A        D/A  A
If I've been on your mind,       you hang on ev'ry word I     say,
                 |Em       Esus4  Em    |Bm
Lose yourself in ___ time            at the mention of my name.
       A  |D   G/D  D      |A          D/A   A
Will I ever know        how it feels to hold you   close
              |Em    Esus4  Em      |Bm                    Asus4  A
And have you tell me            whichever road I choose you'll go?
```

Pre-Chorus 2

Repeat Pre-Chorus 1

Chorus 2

```
              ‖D               G/D  D            |Bm  A/B  Bm
I dare you to let me be yours,        your one and on - ly.
                   |F♯m  Bm/F♯ F♯m           |G    F♯m
I promise I'm worthy            to hold in your arms.
      Em      A     |D          G/D   D
So come on, ___ and give me the chance
                   |Bm            A/B   Bm
To prove I am the one who can
      |F♯m Bm/F♯ F♯m               |G      F♯m  Em  A ‖
Walk that mile            until the end ___ starts.
```

Interlude

```
|Cadd9   |Em7     | D5      | G5        ‖
```

Bridge

‖: Cadd9 |
    I know it ain't easy

|Em7 |
 Giving up your heart.

|D5 |
I know it ain't easy

|G5 :‖
 Giving up your heart. (Nobody's…)

  |Cadd9 |
I know it ain't easy

|Em7 |
 Giving up your heart.

 |D5 |
I know it ain't easy

|Em7 |Asus4 A
 Giving up your heart.

Chorus 3

                        ‖D   G/D D |Bm A/B Bm
So, I dare you to let me be yours ____   your one and on - ly.

                   |F♯m Bm/F♯ F♯m |G   F♯m
I promise I'm worthy   to hold in your arms.

   Em   A |D   G/D D
So come on, ____ and give me the chance

                   |Bm   A/B Bm
To prove I am the one who can

             |F♯m Bm/F♯ F♯m |G   F♯m
Walk that mile   until the end ___ starts.

Em   A |D   G/D D
Come on ___ and give me the chance

                 |Bm   A/B Bm
To prove I am the one who can

      |F♯m Bm/F♯ F♯m |G F♯m Em A |D   ‖
Walk that mile   until the end _____ starts.

Rolling in the Deep

Words and Music by
Adele Adkins and Paul Epworth

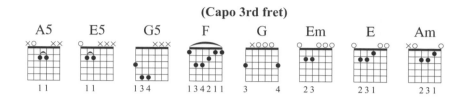

(Capo 3rd fret)

A5   E5   G5   F   G   Em   E   Am

Intro

A5 | | ‖

Verse 1

  A5 | E5 |
There's a fire start - ing in my heart,

     G5 | E5   G5 |
Reach - ing a fever pitch; it's bringing me out the dark.

  A5 | E5 |
Finally I can see you crystal clear.

    G5 | E5   G5   ‖
Go ahead and sell me out and I'll lay your shit bare.

Verse 2

  A5 | E5 |
See how I leave with ever - y piece of you.

    G5 | E5   G5 |
Don't underestimate the things that I will do.

  A5 | E5 |
There's a fire start - ing in my heart,

    G5 | E5   G5   ‖
Reach - ing a fever pitch and it's bringing me out the dark.

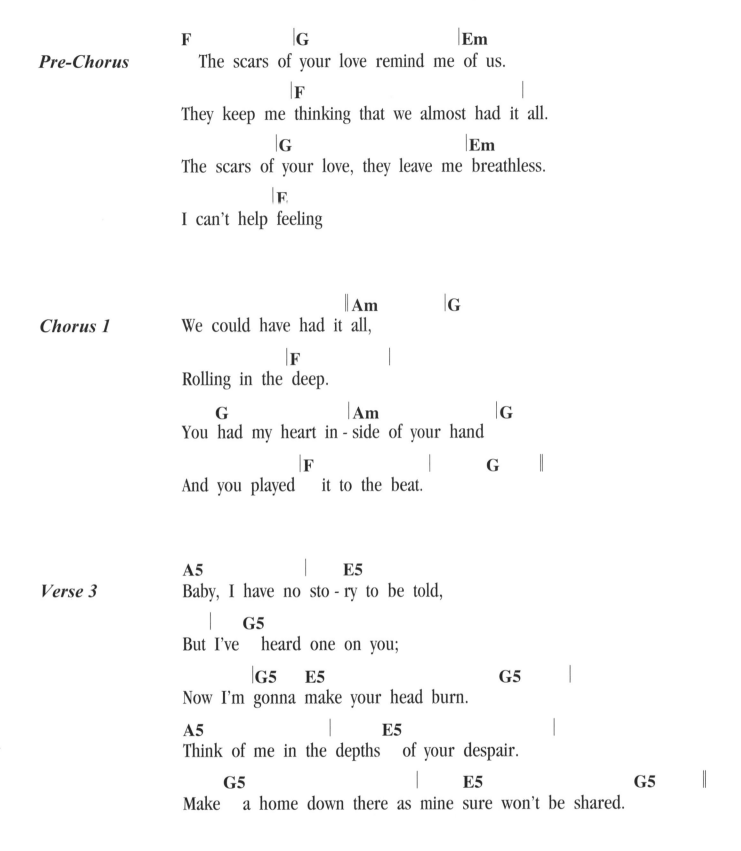

Pre-Chorus

F |G |Em
The scars of your love remind me of us.

        |F |
They keep me thinking that we almost had it all.

      |G |Em
The scars of your love, they leave me breathless.

    |F.
I can't help feeling

Chorus 1

              ‖Am |G
We could have had it all,

     |F |
Rolling in the deep.

   G |Am |G
You had my heart in - side of your hand

       |F | G   ‖
And you played   it to the beat.

Verse 3

A5 | E5
Baby, I have no sto - ry to be told,

  | G5
But I've   heard one on you;

    |G5 E5   G5 |
Now I'm gonna make your head burn.

A5 | E5 |
Think of me in the depths   of your despair.

   G5 | E5   G5   ‖
Make a home down there as mine sure won't be shared.

Repeat Pre-Chorus

Repeat Chorus 1

Chorus 2

G   ‖F |G
We could have had it all,

              |Am |G
Rolling in the deep.

                   |F |
You had my heart in - side of your hand,

              |G | ‖
But you played   it with a beat - ing.

Verse 4

N.C. (A5) | |
Throw your soul through every open door.

                     | |
Count your blessings to find what you look for.

             |
Turn my sorrow into treasured gold.

     | | ‖
You'll pay me back in kind and reap just what you've sown.

Chorus 3

Am |G |F |
             We could have had it all.

  G |Am |G
We could have had it all,

 |F |
It all, it all, it all.

Repeat Chorus 1

Chorus 4

         G   ‖Am |G
We could have had it all,

            |F |
Rolling in the deep.

         G |Am |G
You had my heart in - side of your hand,

            |F |
But you played   it, you played it, you played   it,

            G |Am   ‖
You played   it to the beat.

Set Fire to the Rain

Words and Music by
Adele Adkins and Fraser Smith

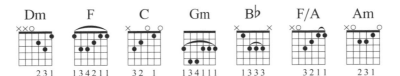

Intro   **Dm**   **F** | |**C**   **Gm** |

Verse 1

‖**Dm** |**F**
I let it fall, my heart,

|**C** |**Gm**
And as it fell you rose to claim   it.

|**Dm** |**F**
It was dark and I was o - ver

|**C** |
Until you kissed my lips and you saved   me.

Verse 2

‖**Dm** |**F**
My hands, they're strong,

|**C** |**Gm**
But my knees were far too weak

|**Dm** |**F**
To stand in your arms

|**C** |
Without fall - ing to your feet.

Pre-Chorus

‖**B♭** |**Gm**
But there's a side to you that I never knew, never knew.

   |**Dm** |
All the things you'd say, they were never true, never true.

   |**B♭** |**C** |
And the games you play, you would always win, always win.

Chorus 1

‖**Dm** |
But I set fire to the rain,

     |**C** |
Watched it pour   as I touched your face.

     |**Gm**
Well, it burned,   well, I cried

     | |**Dm** |**C**
'Cause I heard it screaming out your name, your name!

Verse 3

‖**Dm** |**F**
When I lay with you,

     |**C** |**Gm**
I could stay   there, close   my eyes,

     |**Dm** |**F**
Feel you here   forev - er.

     |**C** |
You and me   together, nothing is bet - ter.

Repeat Pre-Chorus

Repeat Chorus 1

Chorus 2

‖**Dm** |
I set fire to the rain

|**C** |
And I threw us into the flames.

|**Gm**
When it fell,   something died

| |**B♭** |**C**
'Cause I knew that that was the last time, the last time.

Bridge

‖**B♭** |**F/A**
Sometimes I   wake up by the door;

|**Am** |**C**
That heart you caught must be waiting for   you

|**B♭** |**F/A**
Even now   when we're already o - ver,

|**Am** |**C**
I can't help   myself from looking for   you.

Repeat Chorus 1

Repeat Chorus 2

Outro

‖**Dm** | |**C** |
Oh,   oh, no,   oh,

|**Gm** | |**Dm** |**C**
Let it burn,   oh,

|**Dm** | |**C** |
Let it burn,

|**Gm** | |**B♭** |**C** |**NmiCmi**   ‖
Let it burn.

Skyfall
from the Motion Picture SKYFALL

Words and Music by
Adele Adkins and Paul Epworth

(Capo 3rd fret)

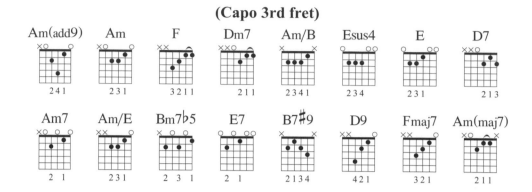

Intro

```
|Am(add9)    |            |
||: Am    F  |Dm7      :|| Play 3 times
|Am/B       |Esus4   E   |
```

Verse 1

```
        ||Am       F  |
This is the end,
|Dm7                  |Am     F        |
   Hold your breath and count ___ to ten.
|Dm7        |Am       F |Dm7
   Feel the earth move and then
              |Am/B    |Esus4   E
Hear my heart burst again.
```

Verse 2

```
        |Am        F  |
For this is the end.
|D7   Dm7                 |Am     F  |
   I've drowned and dreamt this moment.
|D7   Dm7   |Am     F |D7
   So overdue I owe them.
Dm7          |Am/B  |Esus4   E
Swept away, I'm stolen.
```

Chorus 1

‖ Am
Let the sky fall.

Am7 |**F**   **Am/E** |**Dm7**
When it crumbles, we will stand tall,

          |**Bm7♭5**   **E7**
Face it all ____ to - gether.

          |**Am**
Let the sky fall.

Am7 |**F**   **Am/E** |**D7**
When it crumbles we will stand tall,

          |**B7♯9**   **E7** |**Am**   **F** |**D7**
Face it all ____ together at sky - fall.

Dm7 |**Am**   **F** |**D7**
At sky - fall.

Verse 3

Dm7   ‖**Am**   **F** |**D7**
  Skyfall is where ____ we start,

  Dm7 |**Am**   **F** |
A thousand miles and poles apart.

|**D7**   **Dm7** |**Am**   **F**
  Where worlds collide and days are dark.

              |**D7**   **Dm7** |**Am/B**
You may have my number, you can take my name

                              |**Esus4**   **E**
But you'll never have my heart.

Chorus 2

          ‖ **Am**
Let the sky fall.

Am7 |**F**   **Am/E** |**Dm7**
When it crumbles, we will stand tall,

          |**Bm7♭5**   **E7**
Face it all ____ to - gether.

          |**Am**
Let the sky fall.

Am7 |**F**   **Am/E** |**D7**
When it crumbles we will stand tall,

          |**B7♯9**   **E7** |**Am**
Face it all ____ together at sky - fall.

                              |
(Let the sky fall.

| | | |
  When it crumbles, we will stand tall.

| |
  Let the sky fall.

| | |
  When it crumbles,   we will stand tall.)

Bridge

                 ‖D9   **|Fmaj7**
Where you go, I ____ go. What you see, I see.

        |Am7   **Am(maj7)**   **|Am**
I know I'll never be me ___ without the se - curity

Am7   **|Fmaj7**   **Am/E** **|Dm7**
Of your   loving arms keeping me from harm.

               |Am/B   **|**   **E**
Put your hand ___ in my hand and we'll stand.

Chorus 3

        ‖Am
Let the sky fall.

Am7 **|F**   **Am/E** **|Dm7**
When it crumbles, we will stand tall,

        |Bm7♭5 **E7**
Face it all ___ to - gether.

      |Am
Let the sky fall.

Am7 **|F**   **Am/E** **|D7**
When it crumbles we will stand tall,

      |B7♯9   **E7**   **|Am**
Face it all ___ together at sky - fall.

           Am7 **|F Am/E |**
Let the sky fall.

|Dm7   **|Bm7♭5**
  We will stand tall

E7 **|Am Am7** **|F Am/E |D9**   **|E**   **|Am(add9)**   **‖**
At sky - fall,   ooh.

Someone Like You

Words and Music by
Adele Adkins and Dan Wilson

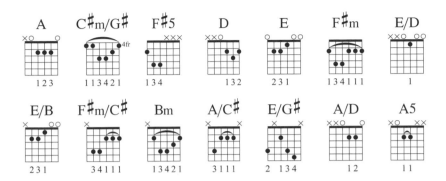

Intro |A |C#m/G# |F#5 |D |

Verse 1 ‖A |C#m/G#
I ___ heard that you're settled down,
|F#5 |D |A
That you found a girl and you're married now.
|C#m/G#
I heard that your dreams came true,
|F#5 |D
Guess she gave you things I didn't give to you.
|A |C#m/G#
Old ___ friend, why are you so ___ shy?
|F#5 |D
Ain't like you to hold back or hide from the light.

Pre-Chorus 1 ‖E F#m
I hate to turn up out of the blue uninvited,
|D
But I ___ couldn't stay away, I couldn't fight it.
|E F#m
I had hoped you'd see my face and that you'd be reminded that,
|D E/D |D |
For me, it isn't over.

Chorus 1

|A   E |F#m7   D
  Never mind, I'll find ___ someone like ___ you.
    |A   E |F#m D
I wish nothing but the best ___ for you, ___ too.
     |A   E |F#m   D
Dont for - get me, I beg. ___ I re - member you said,
       |A   E |F#m D
"Sometimes it lasts in love, but sometimes it hurts in - stead."
     |A   E |F#m |D   ‖
Sometimes it lasts in love, but sometimes it hurts in - stead.

Verse 2

|A |C#m/G#
  You know how the   time flies,
 |F#m |D
Only   yesterday was the time of our lives.
    |A |C#m/G#
We were born and raised in a   summer haze,
  |F#m |D
Bound by the surprise of our glory days.

Pre-Chorus 2

‖E   F#m
I hate to turn up out of the blue uninvited,
   |D
But I ___ couldn't stay away, I couldn't fight it.
   |E   F#m
I had hoped you'd see my face and that you'd be reminded that,
 |D   E/D |D E/D |
For me, it isn't over.

Chorus 2

|A   E |F#m7   D
  Never mind, I'll find ___ someone like ___ you.
    |A   E |F#m D
I wish nothing but the best ___ for you, ___ too.
     |A   E |F#m   D
Don't for - get me, I beg. ___ I re - member you said,
       |A   E |F#m D |
"Sometimes it lasts in love, but sometimes it hurts in - stead."

Bridge

```
|E/B
 Nothing compares, no worries or cares,
    |F♯m/C♯                                    |
Re - grets and mistakes, they're memories made.
|D                            |Bm   A/C♯   |D     E/D  |
 Who would have known how bitter - sweet this would taste?
```

Chorus 3

```
|A                    E              |F♯m7   D
  Never mind, I'll find ___ someone like ___ you.
     |A              E/G♯     |F♯m  D
I wish nothing but the best ___ for you.
        |A          E     |F♯m         D
Don't for - get me, I beg. ___ I re - member you said,
           |A          E/G♯              |F♯m  D    |
"Sometimes it lasts in love, but sometimes it hurts in - stead."
```

Outro-Chorus

```
|A                    E              |F♯m7
  Never mind, I'll find ___ someone like ___ you.
     |A              E        |F♯m  D
I wish nothing but the best ___ for you, ___ too.
        |A          E     |F♯m             D
Don't for - get me, I beg. ___ I re - member you said,
           |A          E              |F♯m  D    |
"Sometimes it lasts in love, but sometimes it hurts in - stead."
           |A
"Sometimes it lasts in love,
    E                    |F♯m  D|E/D  A/D |D     |A5    ‖
But sometimes it hurts in - stead."
```

Turning Tables

Words and Music by
Adele Adkins and Ryan Tedder

(Capo 3rd fret)

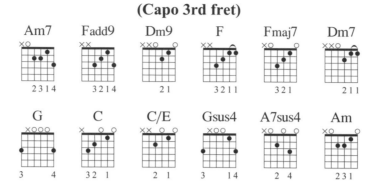

Intro |Am7 |Fadd9 |Dm9 |F Fmaj7 ‖

Verse 1
|Am7 |Fadd9
Close enough to start a war,
    |Dm9 |F   Fmaj7 |
All that I ___ have is on the floor.
|Am7 |Fadd9
God only knows what we're fighting for.
    |Dm9 |F   Fmaj7   ‖
All that I ___ say, you always say ___ more.

Pre-Chorus 1
|F |Dm7
I can't keep up with your turning tables.
    |F |G
Under your thumb, I can't breathe.

Chorus 1
    ‖Am7 Fadd9 |C   Dm7
So I won't let you   close enough to hurt me.
    |Am7 Fadd9 |C   Dm7
No, I won't rescue   you to just de - sert me.
    |Am7 Fadd9 |F   C/E   Gsus4   G
I can't give you _____   the heart you think you gave   me.
    |Dm7 C |F |Am7 |Fadd9
It's time to say   good - bye to turning ta - bles,
    |Dm9 |F Fmaj7 ‖
To turning ta - bles.

Verse 2

```
|Am7                        |Fadd9         |
  Under hardest guise, I see, _____ ooh.
|Dm9                              |F     Fmaj7   |
  Where love is lost, your ghost is found.
|Am7                        |Fadd9
  I braved a hundred storms _____ to leave you.
                    |Dm9                        |F     Fmaj7    ||
As hard as you try, ___ no, I will never be knocked down.
```

Pre-Chorus 2   *Repeat Pre-Chorus 1*

Chorus 2   *Repeat Chorus 1*

Bridge

```
|A7sus4                 |Fadd9              |
  Next time I'll be braver, I'll be my own savior
|C                        |Dm7      |
  When the thunder calls for me.
|A7sus4                 |Fadd9              |
  Next time I'll be braver, I'll be my own savior
|C                        |G          ||
  Standin' on my own two feet.
```

Chorus 3

```
|Am7   Fadd9  |C              Dm7
  I won't let you    close enough to hurt me.
   |Am7   Fadd9  |C              Dm7
No, I won't rescue     you to just de - sert me.
     |Am7     Fadd9 |F            C/E      Gsus4   G
I can't give you _____   the heart you think you gave    me.
        |Dm7  C     F    |              |Am7 |Fadd9
It's time to say    good - bye ___ to turning ta - bles,
             |Dm9   |F      |Am7                  |Fadd9
To turning ta - bles, ___ turning ___ tables, yeah, yeah.
        |Dm9        |F   Fmaj7  |          |Am        ||
From turn - ing, yeah, yeah.
```

When We Were Young

Words and Music by
Adele Adkins and Tobias Jesso Jr.

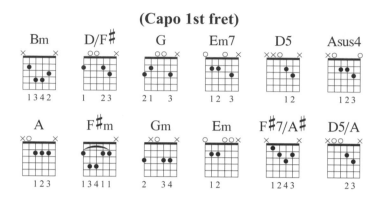

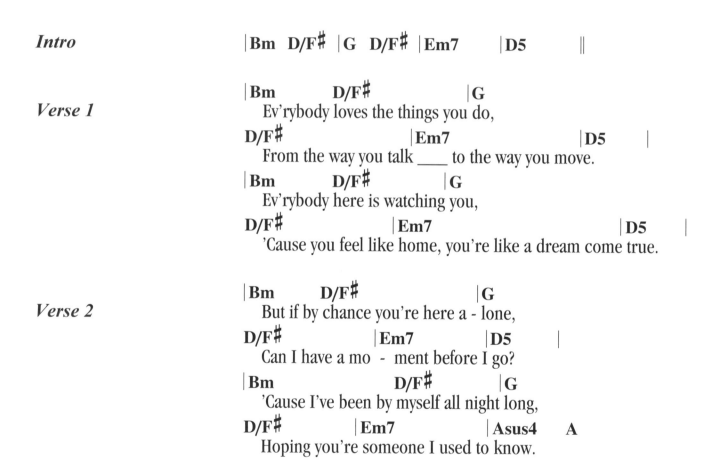

Intro

|Bm D/F♯ |G D/F♯ |Em7 |D5 ||

Verse 1

|Bm   D/F♯ |G
Ev'rybody loves the things you do,
D/F♯ |Em7 |D5 |
From the way you talk ___ to the way you move.
|Bm   D/F♯ |G
Ev'rybody here is watching you,
D/F♯ |Em7 |D5 |
'Cause you feel like home, you're like a dream come true.

Verse 2

|Bm   D/F♯ |G
But if by chance you're here a - lone,
D/F♯ |Em7 |D5 |
Can I have a mo - ment before I go?
|Bm   D/F♯ |G
'Cause I've been by myself all night long,
D/F♯ |Em7 |Asus4   A
Hoping you're someone I used to know.

Pre-Chorus 1

```
                          ‖G    A               |F♯m   G
You look like a mov - ie,    you sound like a song;
                     |            A              |F♯m    A
My God, this re - minds me     of when we were young.
```

Chorus 1

```
                       |D5           D/F♯
Let me pho - tograph you in ___ this light,
                 |G          A             |D5
In case ___ it is the last __ time that we might
       D/F♯                |G           A
Be exact  -  ly like we were __ before we re - alized
                |Bm            D/F♯              |G
We were sad ___ of getting old, ___ it made us rest - less.
Gm                       |Em             |Asus4   A     ‖
   It was just like a mov  -  ie, it was just like a song.
```

Verse 3

```
|Bm         D/F♯          |G
   I was so scared to face my fears,
D/F♯               |Em7                |D5           |
   'Cause nobody told ___ me that you'd be here.
|Bm           D/F♯            |G
   And I swear you'd moved over - seas:
D/F♯              |Em7             |Asus4    A
   That's what you said when you left me.
```

Pre-Chorus 2

```
                          ‖G   A                 |F♯m   G
You still look like a mov - ie,   you still sound like a song;
                     |            A              |F♯m    A
My God, this re - minds me     of when we were young.
```

Chorus 2

|D5   D/F♯
Let me pho - tograph you in ___ this light,

|G   A |D5
In case ___ it is the last __ time that we might

D/F♯ |G   A
Be exact - ly like we were __ before we re - alized

|Bm   D/F♯ |G
We were sad ___ of getting old, ___ it made us rest - less.

Gm |Em |Asus4   F♯7/A♯
It was just like a mov - ie, it was just like a song.

Interlude 1

‖Bm   D5/A |G   D/F♯
(When we __ were young,   when we __ were young,

|Em7 |Asus4   F♯7/A♯
When we ___ were young, when we ___ were young.)

|Bm   D/A
It's hard __ to win __ me there.

|G   D/F♯ |Em7
Ev - 'rything just takes ___ me back to when   you were there,

|Asus4   F♯7/A♯
To when you ____ were there.

|Bm   D/A
And a part __ of me keeps hold - ing on

|G   D/F♯
Just __ in case it has - n't gone.

|Em7
I guess   I still care.

|Asus4   A
Do you ___ still care?

Pre-Chorus 3

```
                              ‖G   A                    |F♯m    G
It was just like a mov - ie,     it was just like a song.
                              |          A                |F♯m    A
My God, this re - minds me     of when we were young.
```

Interlude 2

```
                       |D5            D/F♯        |G              A
(When we __ were young,        when we __ were young,
                       |D5            D/F♯        |G              A
When we __ were young,        when we __ were young.)
```

Outro-Chorus

```
                       ‖D5            D/F♯
Let me pho - tograph you in __ this light,
             |G            A                    |D5
In case __ it is the last __ time that we might
         D/F♯               |G              A
Be exact  - ly like we were __ before we re - alized
                 |Bm          D/F♯              |G      A
We were sad __ of getting old, ___ it made us rest - less.
                 |Bm          D/F♯              |G      Gm
Oh, I'm so mad at getting old, ___ it makes me reck - less.
                        |Em7
It was just like a mov  - ie,
                        |Asus4   A
It was just like a song
                        |D5           ‖
When we were young.
```

STRUM & SING

Lyrics, chord symbols,
and guitar chord diagrams
for your favorite songs.

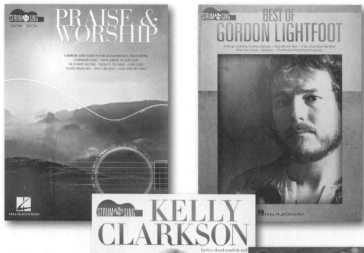

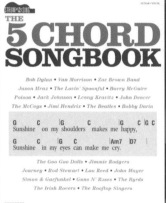

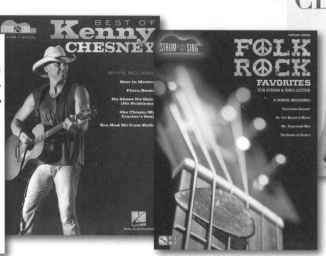

GUITAR

SARA BAREILLES
00102354.................................$12.99

ZAC BROWN BAND
02501620.................................$12.99

COLBIE CAILLAT
02501725.................................$14.99

CAMPFIRE FOLK SONGS
02500686.................................$10.99

CHART HITS OF 2014-2015
00142554.................................$12.99

BEST OF KENNY CHESNEY
00142457.................................$14.99

KELLY CLARKSON
00146384.................................$14.99

JOHN DENVER COLLECTION
02500632...................................$9.95

EAGLES
00157994.................................$12.99

EASY ACOUSTIC SONGS
00125478.................................$12.99

50 CHILDREN'S SONGS
02500825...................................$7.95

THE 5 CHORD SONGBOOK
02501718.................................$10.99

FOLK SONGS
02501482...................................$9.99

FOLK/ROCK FAVORITES
02501669...................................$9.99

40 POP/ROCK HITS
02500633...................................$9.95

THE 4 CHORD SONGBOOK
02501533.................................$12.99

THE 4-CHORD COUNTRY SONGBOOK
00114936.................................$12.99

HITS OF THE '60S
02501138.................................$10.95

HITS OF THE '70S
02500871...................................$9.99

HYMNS
02501125...................................$8.99

JACK JOHNSON
02500858.................................$16.99

CAROLE KING
00115243.................................$10.99

BEST OF GORDON LIGHTFOOT
00139393.................................$14.99

DAVE MATTHEWS BAND
02501078.................................$10.95

JOHN MAYER
02501636.................................$10.99

INGRID MICHAELSON
02501634.................................$10.99

THE MOST REQUESTED SONGS
02501748.................................$10.99

JASON MRAZ
02501452.................................$14.99

PRAISE & WORSHIP
00152381.................................$12.99

ROCK AROUND THE CLOCK
00103625.................................$12.99

ROCK BALLADS
02500872...................................$9.95

ED SHEERAN
00152016.................................$12.99

THE 6 CHORD SONGBOOK
02502277.................................$10.99

CAT STEVENS
00116827.................................$10.99

TODAY'S HITS
00119301.................................$10.99

KEITH URBAN
00118558.................................$12.99

NEIL YOUNG – GREATEST HITS
00138270.................................$12.99

UKULELE

COLBIE CAILLAT
02501731.................................$10.99

JOHN DENVER
02501694.................................$10.99

JACK JOHNSON
02501702.................................$15.99

JOHN MAYER
02501706.................................$10.99

INGRID MICHAELSON
02501741.................................$10.99

THE MOST REQUESTED SONGS
02501453.................................$14.99

JASON MRAZ
02501753.................................$14.99

SING-ALONG SONGS
02501710.................................$14.99

www.halleonard.com
Visit our website to see full song lists.

7777 W. Bluemound Rd. P.O. Box 13819 Milwaukee, WI 53213

Prices, content, and availability subject to change without notice.

0316